We Believe & Celebrate
First PENANCE

The Ad Hoc Committee to Oversee the Use of the Catechism, United States Conference of Catholic Bishops, has found this catechetical text, copyright 2006, to be in conformity, as supplemental catechetical material, with the *Catechism of the Catholic Church*.

Sadlier
A Division of William H. Sadlier, Inc.

Sadlier's *We Believe & Celebrate* program was developed by the community of faith through representatives with expertise in liturgy, theology, Scripture, catechesis, and children's faith development. This program leads to a deeper experience of Jesus in the community and springs from the wisdom of this community.

Catechetical and Liturgical Consultants

Dr. Gerard F. Baumbach
Director, Center for Catechetical Initiatives
Concurrent Professor of Theology
University of Notre Dame

Sr. Janet Baxendale, SC
Adjunct Professor of Liturgy
St. Joseph Seminary, Dunwoodie, NY

Carole M. Eipers, D.Min.
Executive Director of Catechetics
William H. Sadlier, Inc.

Rev. Ronald J. Lewinski, S.T.L.
St. Mary of the Annunciation
Mundelein, IL

Rev. Msgr. James P. Moroney
Executive Director of the USCCB
Secretariat for the Liturgy

Curriculum and Child Development Consultants

Patricia Andrews
Director of Religious Education
Our Lady of Lourdes
Slidell, LA

William Bischoff
Director of Catechetical Ministries
Mission San Luis Rey Parish
Oceanside, CA

Diana Carpenter
Director of Faith Formation
St. Elizabeth Ann Seton Parish
San Antonio, TX

Inculturation Consultants

Dulce M. Jimenez-Abreu
Director of Spanish Programs
William H. Sadlier, Inc.

Vilma Angulo
Director of Religious Education
All Saints Catholic Church
Sunrise, FL

Media/Technology Consultant

Sister Jane Keegan, RDC
Senior Internet Editor
William H. Sadlier, Inc.

Theological Consultants

Most Reverend Edward K. Braxton,
    Ph.D., S.T.D.
Official Theological Consultant
Bishop of Belleville

Monsignor John Arnold
Vicar General
Archdiocese of Westminster

Sadlier Consulting Team

Roy Arroyo
Michaela Burke
Judith Devine
Ken Doran
Kathleen Hendricks
William M. Ippolito
Saundra Kennedy, Ed.D.
Kathleen Krane
Suzan Larroquette

Writing/Development Team

Rosemary K. Calicchio
Vice President of Publications

Melissa Gibbons
Product Director

Blake Bergen
Editorial Director

MaryAnn Trevaskiss
Supervising Editor

Maureen Gallo
Senior Editor

Joanna Dailey
Editor

Publishing Operations Team

Deborah J. Jones
Vice President of Publishing Operations

Vince Gallo
Creative Director

Francesca O'Malley
Associate Art Director

Jim Saylor
Photography Manager

Design Staff
Andrea Brown
Sasha Khorovsky
Dmitry Kushnirsky

Production Staff
Barbara Brown
Maureen Morgan
Gavin Smith
Kristine Walsh
Sommer Zakrzewski

Photo Credits

Cover Title Page: Neal Farris.
Interior: Jane Bernard: 18 *right*, 25, 26, 27, 48, 49, 50, 60, 61, 62, 63, 64 *top*, 65 *bottom left*, 80, 84 *top & center*, 88, 90, 95. Crosiers/Gene Plaisted, OSC: 24; 84 *bottom*. Neal Farris: 12, 13, 14, 15, 18 *left*, 30, 37, 42, 54, 64 *bottom*, 66, 72, 74, 75, 78, 82, 86 *center*, 92, 93 *left*, 94, 96. Getty Images/Digital Vision: 36 *top*; Photodisc Red: 36 *bottom*, 86 *bottom*; Brand X Pictures: 38, 93 *right*; Photodisc Green: 39, 86 *top*. Ken Karp: 6. Masterfile/ Kevin Dodge: 31; Ariel Skelley: 67. Punchstock/Creatas: 65 *top*. Superstock/ Kwame Zikomo: 7. Veer/ Stockbyte: 19, 65 *bottom right*; Image Source: 43; Rubberball: 55. W. P. Wittman Limited: 51.

Illustrator Credits

Dan Andreason: 56–57. Tom Barrett: 72–73. Sara Beise: 53. Mary Bono: 8, 18, 40, 53, 56, 78. Mircea Catusanu: 28, 29, 96. Mark Graham: 8–9. Layne Johnson: 32–33. W.B. Johnston: 6, 12, 14, 25, 26, 37–39, 41, 48–51, 63, 88, 95. Dave Jonason: 44, 45, 54, 68, 69. Kathleen Kemley: 68–69. Daryl Ligason: 20–21. Dean MacAdam: 20, 40, 41, 56, 57, 69. Diana Magnuson: 10–11, 22–23, 34–35, 46–47, 58–59, 70–71, 81, 83, 85, 87, 89, 91, 94. Ariel Pang: 20. Gary Phillips: 4–5. Mike Reed: 44–45. Jackie Snider: 21, 30, 76, 77, 92. Jessica Wolk-Stanley: 86, 92.

Nihil Obstat
✠ Most Reverend Robert C. Morlino

Imprimatur
✠ Most Reverend Robert C. Morlino
Bishop of Madison
November 10, 2005

The *Nihil Obstat* and *Imprimatur* are official declarations that a book or pamphlet is free of doctrinal or moral error. No implication is contained therein that those who have granted the *Nihil Obstat* and *Imprimatur* agree with the contents, opinions, or statements expressed.

Acknowledgments

Scripture excerpts are taken from the *New American Bible with Revised New Testament and Psalms*. Copyright © 1991, 1986, 1970, Confraternity of Christian Doctrine, Inc., Washington, D.C. Used with permission. All rights reserved. No portion of the *New American Bible* may be reprinted without permission in writing from the copyright owner.

Excerpts from the English translation of *Rite of Penance* © 1974, International Committee on English in the Liturgy, Inc. (ICEL). All rights reserved.

English translation of the Glory to the Father and Lord's Prayer by the International Consultation on English Texts (ICET).

"We Celebrate with Joy," © 2000, Carey Landry. Published by OCP Publications, 5536 NE Hassalo, Portland, OR 97213. All rights reserved. Used with permission. "The Good Shepherd," text and music © 1994, Paule Freeburg, DC and Christopher Walker. Published by OCP Publications, 5536 NE Hassalo, Portland OR 97213. All rights reserved. Used with permission. "Children of God," © 1991, Christopher Walker. Published by OCP Publications, 5536 NE Hassalo, Portland, OR 97213. All rights reserved. Used with permission. "Jesus Wants to Help Us," music and text © 1999, Christopher Walker and Paule Freeburg, DC. Published by OCP Publications, 5536 NE Hassalo, Portland, OR 97213. All rights reserved. Used with permission. "We Come to Ask Forgiveness," © 1986, Carey Landry and North American Liturgy Resources. All rights reserved. "God Has Made Us a Family," © 1986, Carey Landry and North American Liturgy Resources (NALR), 5536 NE Hassalo, Portland, OR 97213. All rights reserved. Used with permission.

Printed on acid-free paper

Welcome to
We Believe & Celebrate

Your **We Believe & Celebrate** First Penance and First Communion student books are printed on acid-free paper so they can become true keepsakes. Artwork and photos can be taped to this paper with long-lasting results and will never yellow or fade. Markers will not bleed or show through the pages.

To enhance your **We Believe & Celebrate** scrapbooking experience:

◆ Use darker colored pencils, soft lead pencils, and dark colored crayons.

◆ Suggested markers include: Faber-Castell 24 Washable Fineline Markers, Crayola 20 Super Tips Washable Markers, Roseart 30 Washable Super Tip Markers, and Loew-Cornell 24 Fine Point Markers.

◆ Try the very popular technique of drawing and writing with crayons, colored pencils, and markers on separate sheets of paper and then affix to text pages.

◆ Children love to scrapbook with stickers, stencils, and wallpaper. Download our free stickers, stencils, and wallpaper at **www.webelieveandcelebrate.com.**

◆ Print stickers and wallpaper on sheets of 8 1/2 x 11 inch Avery #5165 (or comparable) self-adhesive paper or on normal paper and then affix to text pages.

◆ Visit **www.webelieveandcelebrate.com** for more scrapbooking tips and tips for completing keepsake pages.

Enjoy this time of preparation!

CONTENTS

4

In our church there are different places where we might go to confession.

5

Welcome!

We Believe & Celebrate First Penance is your book. You will use it to prepare for First Penance. Many people will guide you as you learn about this special celebration in your life. So make this book one that you can keep forever.

As you go through each chapter you will:

✦ **Gather and Share God's Word**

You celebrate the people and things in your life. You read and listen to a story from the Bible.

✦ **Believe and Celebrate**

You learn about and prepare to receive the Sacrament of Penance.

✦ **Respond and Pray**

With your family and friends you remember and celebrate what you believe. You celebrate your love for God in words and song.

Let's get Started!

We Are Followers of Jesus

"This I command you:
love one another."

John 15:17

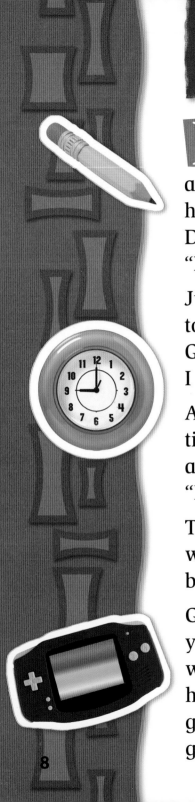

Dan went to his Grandma Lynn's house after school. Grandma Lynn asked Dan to do his homework before he played video games. Dan asked, "Why?" Grandma answered, "Because I love you."

Just before dinner Grandma reminded Dan to wash his hands. Again Dan asked, "Why?" Grandma gave the same answer, "Because I love you."

At 9:00 P.M. Grandma said, "Dan, now it's time for you to go to sleep." When Dan asked Grandma why, she answered, "Because I love you."

Then Dan smiled and asked, "Grandma, why do you keep saying everything is because you love me?"

Grandma said, "Well, I wanted you to do your homework because I want you to do well in school. I asked you to wash your hands because I don't want you to eat with germs on your hands. That is how people get sick."

"If you go to sleep now, you won't be tired for school.
I asked you to do all these things because I care about you.
I want you to be safe and happy."

Dan looked at Grandma Lynn and said,

"_____

_____."
(fill in your answer)

Here is someone who cares about and protects me.

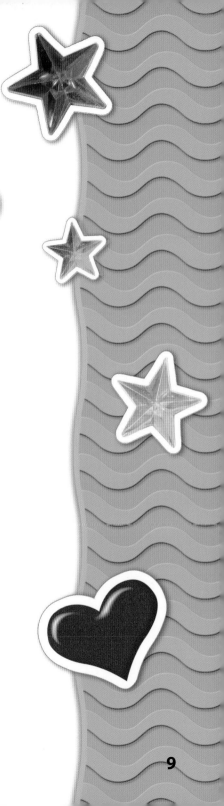

9

We Share God's Word

Narrator: We believe in the Blessed Trinity, three Persons in one God: God the Father, God the Son, God the Holy Spirit. Jesus is God the Son. He taught that God the Father loves us and protects us by giving us laws. Jesus taught us that the Holy Spirit would help us to follow God's laws.

God's laws are called commandments. Jesus taught us that by following the commandments we show our love for God, ourselves, and others.

 Matthew 22:35–39

Reader: Jesus went from town to town to tell people about God's love. One day someone asked Jesus which commandment is the greatest. Jesus said, "You shall love the Lord, your God, with all your heart, with all your soul, and with all your mind." Then he said, "You shall love your neighbor as yourself." (Matthew 22:37, 39)

We call this teaching of Jesus the Great Commandment.

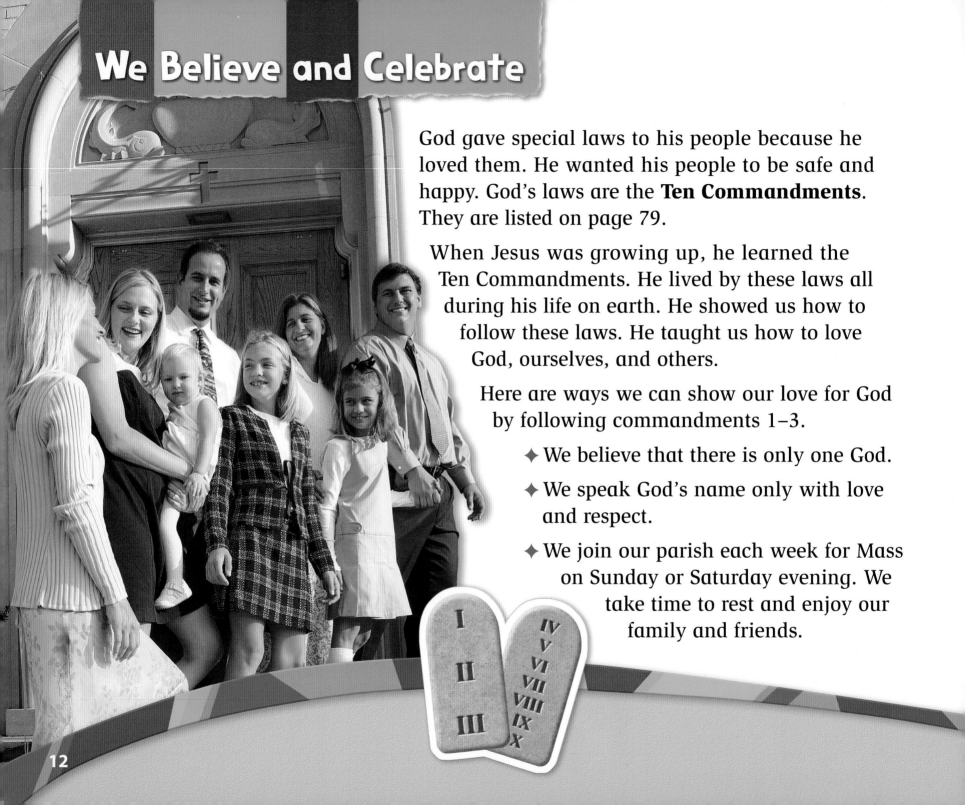

We Believe and Celebrate

God gave special laws to his people because he loved them. He wanted his people to be safe and happy. God's laws are the **Ten Commandments**. They are listed on page 79.

When Jesus was growing up, he learned the Ten Commandments. He lived by these laws all during his life on earth. He showed us how to follow these laws. He taught us how to love God, ourselves, and others.

Here are ways we can show our love for God by following commandments 1–3.

✦ We believe that there is only one God.

✦ We speak God's name only with love and respect.

✦ We join our parish each week for Mass on Sunday or Saturday evening. We take time to rest and enjoy our family and friends.

Here are ways we can show love for ourselves and others by following commandments 4–10.

✦ We listen to and obey our parents and all those who care for us.

✦ We respect all human life. We do not fight or hurt anyone.

✦ We respect our own bodies and the bodies of others.

✦ We take care of what we have. We do not steal what other people have.

✦ We tell the truth.

✦ We show that we are thankful for our family and friends.

✦ We show that we are thankful for what we have. We share what we have with others.

Remember that Jesus' teaching about loving God, ourselves, and others is called the **Great Commandment**. When we follow the Great Commandment, we follow all of God's commandments. We live as God's children.

We Believe and Celebrate

Jesus taught us to show love for God, ourselves, and others. God wants us to choose to obey his laws as Jesus taught us to do. Yet God never forces us to obey his commandments. God gives us the gift of **free will**. This gift allows us to make choices.

God lets us use our free will to follow his laws or not to follow his laws. God allows us to choose to love and respect him, ourselves, and others.

God has also given us a gift to help us make the right choices. God has given us a conscience. Our **conscience** helps us to know what is right and what is wrong, what to do and what not to do. Our conscience helps us to obey God's commandments.

Sometimes people choose to turn away from God's love. They decide not to follow God's law. When they do this they hurt their friendship with God.

But it is important to remember that God always loves us. God is always ready to forgive us if we are sorry. God always gives us the grace to do what he commands. And we can always pray to God the Holy Spirit to help us make the right choices.

Making Choices

Every day we make choices. Sometimes we have a choice between obeying or not obeying one of the commandments. Before we make a choice, we should stop and think. We should ask ourselves these questions before we choose:

- If I do this, will I show love for God, myself, or others?
- What would Jesus want me to do?

There are some things that we must never choose because they are always wrong, or evil. We must never choose these things even if we think good might come from them.

We Respond

This week I can join my parish community to show love for God.

Here is one way I will do this...

Here is one way my family can show love and respect for one another this week ...

Here is one way my family can show love and respect for our neighbors ...

We Respond in Prayer

† **Leader:** Lord God, we gather together to celebrate your love for us. We thank you for giving us your laws. We ask you to help us follow these laws at all times and in all places.

All: "The earth, LORD, is filled with
    your love;
        teach me your laws." (Psalm 119:64)

Leader: Lord God, in the Bible we read about your commandments. We learn the teachings of Jesus about showing our love for you, ourselves, and others. We learn that the Holy Spirit is with us to help us make good choices.

All: "The earth, LORD, is filled with
    your love;
        teach me your laws." (Psalm 119:64)

Leader: Let us sing together about God's love.

♫ **We Celebrate with Joy**

Chorus
We celebrate with joy and gladness!
We celebrate God's love for us!
We celebrate with joy and gladness:
God with us today!
God with us today!

God surrounding us;
God surprising us;
God in everything we do!
God surrounding us;
God surprising us;
God in all we do!

(Chorus)

We Remember God's Love and Forgiveness

2

"The LORD is my shepherd."

Psalm 23:1

We Gather

Last week Marta Cruz, her dad, and her brother Carlos went to Parktown's Family Festival. On their way there, Mr. Cruz said, "The festival is going to be very crowded. I want you to stay close to me at all times."

First the family stopped at the craft stands. They looked at the beautiful things people had made. Both Mr. Cruz and Carlos wanted to take time to look at everything.

Marta thought, "This is so boring. I want to do something else." Marta saw her friend, Jenny, on the festival shuttle. Marta waved. The shuttle stopped close to where Marta was standing. She hopped on and sat next to Jenny.

When Mr. Cruz noticed that Marta was not beside him, he was worried. He asked Carlos, "Where is Marta?" They looked up and saw Marta on the shuttle. The driver was just pulling away. Mr. Cruz said, "Hurry, Carlos! I think we can catch the shuttle."

Carlos and his dad ran. They reached the shuttle just as it stopped near the amusement rides. Mr. Cruz told Marta to get off the shuttle. He said, "Marta, what were you thinking? Carlos and I were really upset when we thought we lost you. We love you and we don't want to get separated from you again!"

Marta was happy to be with her family again. They celebrated by

_____

_____ .

(fill in your answer)

Here is one thing my family likes to do together.

We Share God's Word

Jesus told stories to teach people about God's love. He talked about things his followers knew about. One day Jesus told this story.

 Luke 15:4–6

Reader 1: There was a shepherd who took care of a flock of one hundred sheep. One day one of the sheep wandered away from the flock.

Reader 2: When the shepherd found out the sheep was missing, he left the other ninety-nine sheep. He searched and searched until he found the lost sheep.

Reader 3: The shepherd was very happy that he found the lost sheep. He put the sheep on his shoulders and carried it home.

Reader 4: When the shepherd reached home, he called together his friends and neighbors. He said, "Rejoice with me because I have found my lost sheep." (Luke 15:6)

Jesus told this story to help his followers to understand God's love and forgiveness. He wanted us to know that every one of us is special to God.

We Believe and Celebrate

God loves each of us very much. He wants us to stay as close to him as possible. But this is not always easy to do.

The first humans did something they knew was wrong. They sinned and lost their share in God's life. That first sin is called **original sin**. And ever since then, all people are born with original sin. Because of original sin, suffering and death came into the world. Also, people sometimes find it difficult to do what God wants.

Sometimes we do not show our love for God, ourselves, and others. We choose not to obey God's commandments. We sin. **Sin** is any thought, word, or act that we freely choose to commit even though we know that it is wrong.

When we sin we turn away from God and one another. But Jesus leads us by showing us ways to come back together again.

Jesus said, "I am the good shepherd." (John 10:14) Jesus, our Good Shepherd, leads us to reconciliation with God and others. The word *reconciliation* comes from a word that means "coming back together again."

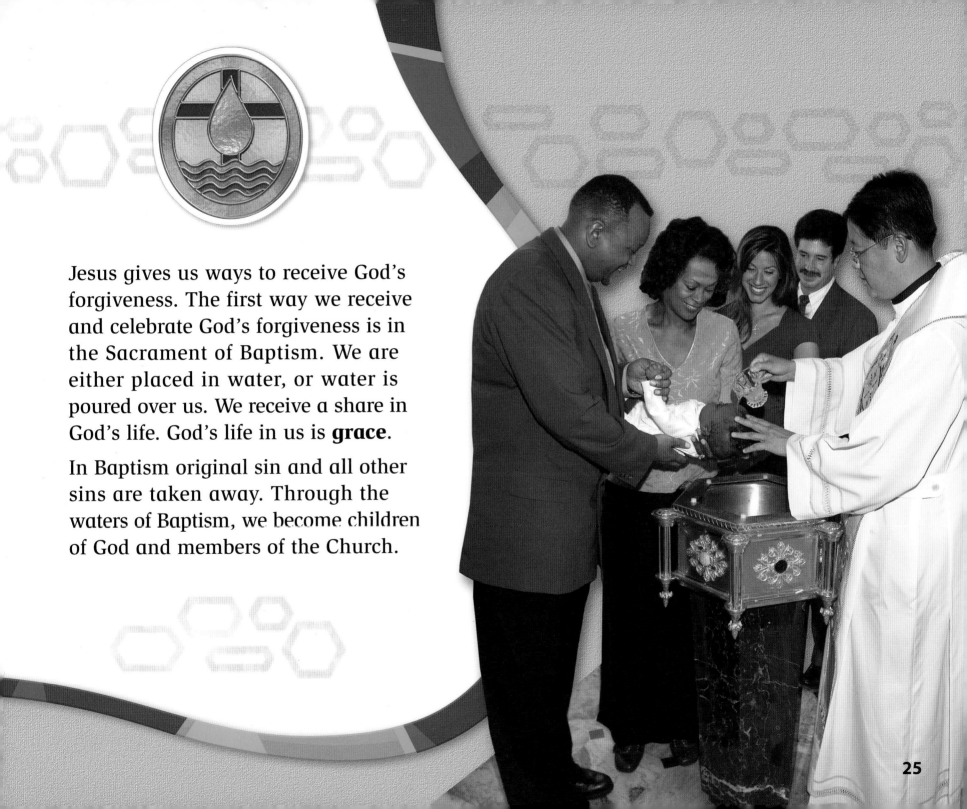

Jesus gives us ways to receive God's forgiveness. The first way we receive and celebrate God's forgiveness is in the Sacrament of Baptism. We are either placed in water, or water is poured over us. We receive a share in God's life. God's life in us is **grace**.

In Baptism original sin and all other sins are taken away. Through the waters of Baptism, we become children of God and members of the Church.

After we are baptized, there are many times in our lives when we need to ask God to forgive us. We can do this in the Sacrament of Penance and Reconciliation. In this sacrament, which we can call the Sacrament of Penance, we ask God for and receive his forgiveness of our sins.

Some sins are more serious than others. These are called mortal sins. To commit a mortal sin, a person knows it is very seriously wrong and freely chooses to commit it anyway. People who commit mortal sin break their friendship with God. They no longer share in God's grace. People who commit mortal sins must receive God's forgiveness in the Sacrament of Penance.

Venial sin is less serious than mortal sin. People who commit venial sin hurt their friendship with God. But they still share in God's grace.

Yet any sin which we commit hurts our friendship with God and others. So we should ask for God's forgiveness for all of our sins in the Sacrament of Penance.

When We Celebrate

We celebrate the sacrament of forgiveness. It is also called the:

- sacrament of conversion
- Sacrament of Penance
- sacrament of confession
- Sacrament of Reconciliation.

Children who are baptized as infants must celebrate the Sacrament of Penance for the first time before their First Holy Communion.

We Respond

Jesus wants me to share his stories about God's love and forgiveness.

Here is one story that I can share ...

My family can pray to Jesus, our Good Shepherd.

Here is my family's prayer …

We Respond in Prayer

✝ **Leader:** Jesus, through the Sacraments of Baptism and Penance, we share in God's love, and we receive and celebrate God's forgiveness. Thank you for these sacraments.

All: Jesus, we thank you for sharing God's love and forgiveness.

Leader: Jesus, you told us that you are our Good Shepherd. We believe that you never want us to be separated from you.

All: Jesus, you are our Good Shepherd. We are the sheep of your flock.

Leader: Let us now sing to Jesus, our Good Shepherd.

♫ The Good Shepherd

Jesus is the Good Shepherd,
   he knows his sheep and he loves them.
Jesus is the Good Shepherd;
   he loves us all, he loves us all.

Jesus calls our name:

(Sing your name two times.)
   and we come to him
   running and running and
     running and running
   and running and running
     because we love him.

30

We Prepare to Receive God's Forgiveness

3

"May God open your hearts to his law."

Rite of Penance

We Gather

Last Saturday morning Lisa was getting ready to go to the library. Andrew asked, "Where are you going, Lisa? Can I go, too?"

Lisa answered, "Not today. Kelly and I are going to work on our project for nature scouts. It's about seashells. If our group leader likes our project, Kelly and I will get our nature badges."

Andrew was angry when Lisa left without him. He went into her room and found her favorite seashell. Andrew thought, "Lisa probably wanted to use this shell for her project. Well, she won't be able to use it now. I'm going to hide it in my room."

At dinner that night, Lisa was excited because she had found five books about seashells. Lisa told Andrew that she would show him the books after dinner. She explained, "I'm going to use shells from my collection for the project. Just wait until my group leader sees my favorite shell. Nature badge, you are mine!"

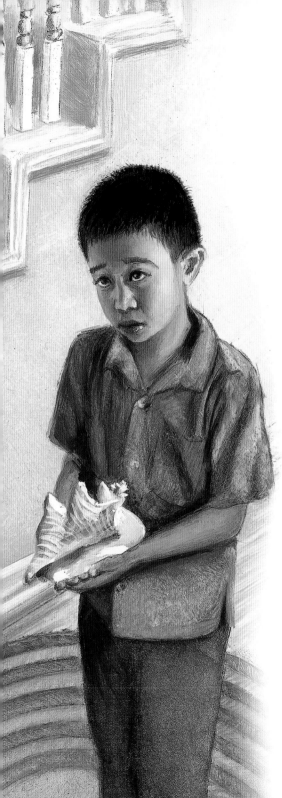

Andrew felt awful. He thought, "I was being selfish this afternoon. Lisa really wants to get that nature badge. I shouldn't have taken her shell."

So after dinner Andrew went and got the shell. He handed it to Lisa. He said,

" _____

_____ ."

(fill in your answer)

Here are ways I can say "I'm sorry."

33

Jesus told this story to help us to understand God's love and forgiveness.

 Luke 15:11–24

There was a loving father who had two sons. One day the younger son asked for his share of the family's money. The father gave it to him. The son left home. He spent all his money with his friends. When it was gone, his friends left him. He had no place to live and no money to buy clothes or food.

The son thought about his selfish choices. He remembered his father's love. He decided to go home and ask his father for forgiveness.

When the young man was almost home, his father saw him on the road. The father ran out to welcome his son. The young man said, "Father, I have sinned.... I no longer deserve to be called your son." (Luke 15:21)

The father was very happy to see his son. The father loved and forgave his son. He gathered the family for a celebration.

We Believe and Celebrate

In Jesus' story about the father and son, the son was not happy or peaceful. After he spent all his money, he thought about the choices he had made. He knew that many of his choices were selfish.

We, too, should think about whether or not our choices show love for God, ourselves, and others. When we do this we make an **examination of conscience**.

As we prepare to celebrate the Sacrament of Penance, we make an examination of conscience. When we make an examination of conscience, we do the following things.

+ We ask the Holy Spirit to help us remember the choices we have made.

+ We think about the ways we have or have not followed the Ten Commandments.

+ We ask ourselves questions to help us remember what we have thought, said, or done.

+ We ask ourselves if there were times we could have done good for others but did not.

Here are some questions you can ask when you examine your conscience.

Ask Yourself

Respect for God

✦ Did I take time to pray?

✦ Did I speak God's name in the right way?

Respect for Myself

✦ Did I take care of my body?

✦ Did I give thanks for all the gifts God has given me?

Respect for Others

✦ Did I obey my parents and all those who care for me?

✦ Did I hurt other people by what I said or did?

✦ Did I look for ways to help others?

In Jesus' story about the father and son, the son felt sorrow for the wrong choices he had made. Another word for sorrow is *contrition*.

We pray a special prayer to tell God that we are sorry for the wrong choices we have made. We call this prayer an *act of contrition*.

We pray an act of contrition during the Sacrament of Penance.

I am sorry

Here is one act of contrition that we can pray. You can prepare for the sacrament by learning this prayer.

Act of Contrition

My God,
I am sorry for my sins with
    all my heart.
In choosing to do wrong
and failing to do good,
I have sinned against you
whom I should love above all things.
I firmly intend, with your help,
to do penance,
to sin no more,
and to avoid whatever leads me to sin.
Our Savior Jesus Christ
suffered and died for us.
In his name, my God, have mercy.

When We Pray

The following words are in the Act of Contrition on this page. This is what we are telling God when we pray them.

- "firmly intend"—We really mean to do what we promise.
- "do penance"—We will do something to make up for the wrong choices we have made.
- "have mercy"—We ask for God's love and forgiveness.

Here is a place where I can examine my conscience . . .

A time when I can examine my conscience . . .

Our family plan for showing respect for God, myself, and others is . . .

We Respond in Prayer

✝ **Leader:** God, thank you for always being ready to forgive us.

All: My God,
I am sorry for my sins with all my heart.
In choosing to do wrong
and failing to do good,
I have sinned against you
whom I should love above all things.
I firmly intend, with your help,
to do penance,
to sin no more,
and to avoid whatever leads
  me to sin.
Our Savior Jesus Christ
suffered and died for us.
In his name, my God,
  have mercy.

Leader: Let us celebrate God's love and forgiveness in song.

♫ Children of God

Chorus
Children of God in one family,
  loved by God in one family.
And no matter what we do
  God loves me and God loves you.

Jesus teaches us to love.
Sometimes we get it wrong.
But God forgives us every time
  for we belong to the (Chorus)

Jesus wants us to be sorry.
Sometimes we get it wrong.
But God forgives us
  every time
  for we belong to the (Chorus)

4

We Prepare to Celebrate Penance

"May the Lord guide your hearts."

Rite of Penance

We Gather

Last Tuesday Margaret was upset. Her mother asked, "What's wrong, Margaret?"

Margaret said, "Our class is going to have a play about exploring space. Everyone tried out for the role of the captain of the space station. Our teacher picked Ellie for the part."

Margaret's mother asked, "Aren't you happy for Ellie? I thought she was your best friend."

Margaret answered, "Ellie is my best friend. But I was jealous. I didn't talk to Ellie at the lunch table or outside in the yard. Now I'm sorry that I hurt Ellie. What do you think I should do?"

Margaret's mother thought for a minute. Then she said, "I think you should tell Ellie you are sorry. If you want to, you can call her now."

Margaret called Ellie. Margaret said, "I'm sorry, Ellie."
Ellie forgave Margaret. Margaret showed she was
sorry by

_____

_____.

(fill in your answer)

**Here is a way that I can show a friend that
I am sorry.**

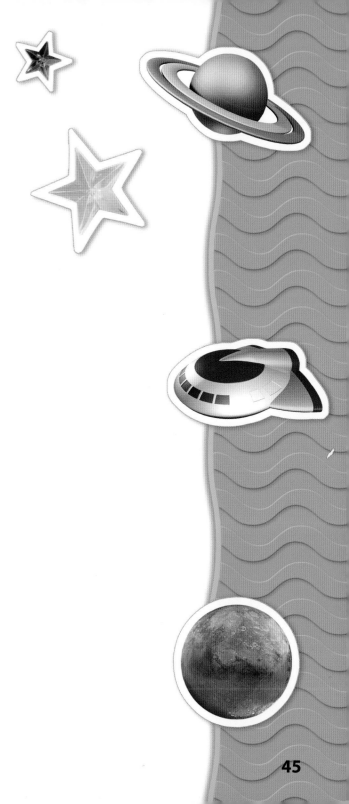

📖 Luke 19:1–10

Reader 1: One day a crowd gathered to see Jesus. Zacchaeus, a rich tax collector, was in the crowd. He wanted to see Jesus but was too short to see over the crowd. So he climbed a tree and waited.

Reader 2: As Jesus walked by the tree, he looked up. He said, "Zacchaeus, come down quickly, for today I must stay at your house."
(Luke 19:5)

Reader 3: Zacchaeus climbed down. He welcomed Jesus to his home. Some people were upset that Jesus went to the tax collector's house. They thought Zacchaeus had cheated them. They did not know why Jesus was visiting this man.

Reader 4: Then Zacchaeus told Jesus that he would pay back four times the amount of money he owed to people. He would also give half of what he owned to people in need.

Reader 5: Zacchaeus showed by his words and actions that he was really sorry. Jesus told him that he was saved.

We Believe and Celebrate

When Jesus traveled from town to town, he met many people. He shared God's love and forgiveness with them. He forgave people's sins. He celebrated their reconciliation with God and others. Jesus gave us a way to celebrate our reconciliation with God and others, too. He gave us the Sacrament of Penance.

When we celebrate the Sacrament of Penance, we meet with a priest. The priest is acting in Jesus' name. We may sit and face the priest, or we may kneel behind a screen. The priest may read a story from the Bible with us. Then he talks to us about what we can do to make right choices.

In the Sacrament of Penance we tell God that we are sorry for our sins and we promise not to sin again. This is **contrition**. Perfect contrition is being sorry for our sins because we believe in God and love him.

When we tell our sins to the priest, we confess our sins. This part of the sacrament is called **confession**. The priest will never tell anyone the sins that we confess.

During this sacrament, the priest tells us ways we can show God we are sorry. The priest may tell us to say an extra prayer or prayers. He may tell us to do kind acts for others. A prayer or kind act we do to show God we are sorry is **a penance**.

In the Gospel story about Zacchaeus, we find that Zacchaeus promised Jesus that he would show God he was sorry for his sins. We, too, show God that we are sorry for our sins by doing the penance that the priest gives us. We usually do the penance after the celebration of the sacrament.

We Believe and Celebrate

After Jesus rose from the dead, he returned to his Apostles and gave them the power to forgive sin in his name. And today, in the Sacrament of Penance, bishops and priests forgive our sins in Jesus' name. They received this power in the Sacrament of Holy Orders.

God forgives our sins through the words and actions of the priest in the Sacrament of Penance. This is called **absolution**. The word *absolution* comes from a word that means "taking away." When we receive absolution, our sins are taken away.

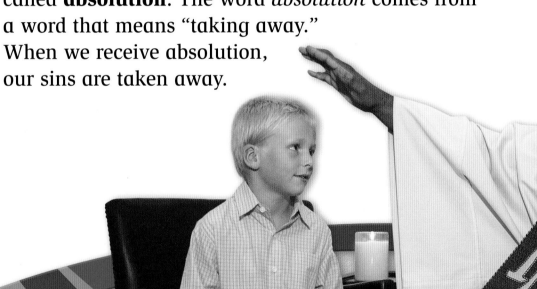

When the priest gives absolution, he stretches his right hand over each person's head and prays:

"God, the Father of mercies,
through the death and resurrection
    of his Son
has reconciled the world to himself
and sent the Holy Spirit among us
for the forgiveness of sins;
through the ministry of the Church
may God give you pardon and peace,
and I absolve you from your sins
in the name of the Father,
    and of the Son, †
and of the Holy Spirit."

We each respond, "Amen."

When We Celebrate

These are the four parts of the Sacrament of Penance:

- contrition
- confession
- a penance
- absolution.

We Respond

When I am forgiven I ...

Our family can celebrate forgiveness by ...

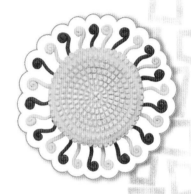

We Respond in Prayer

♫ Jesus Wants to Help Us

We believe Jesus wants to help us.
We believe Jesus wants to help us.
We believe that Jesus always wants to
 help us.

When we pray, Jesus wants to hear us.
When we pray, Jesus wants to hear us.
We believe that Jesus always wants to
 hear us.

✝ Quiet Prayer

Close your eyes. Be very still.
Breathe in. Breathe out.
Remember that Jesus is with you.
He loves you very much.

Talk with Jesus. Tell him ways you have
or have not shown love for

✦ God (Pause)

✦ yourself (Pause)

✦ others. (Pause)

Now tell Jesus the ways you will show
you are sorry for the wrong choices you
have made.

5

We Celebrate Penance with the Church

"Hear us, Lord, for you are merciful and kind."

Rite of Penance

We Gather

This was the day the Santos twins were going to celebrate the Sacrament of Penance for the first time. At breakfast Luz said, "I hope I remember everything I'm supposed to do."

Luz's twin brother Marcos answered, "Don't worry, Luz. Father Michael told us that he would help us."

The twins' mother and father helped them practice the Act of Contrition until it was time to leave for church. When the twins went outside, their grandfather was sitting in the car. Luz said, "Abuelo, I'm so glad you are going with us. We'll teach you one of our songs on the way to church. We're going to sing

_____."

(fill in your answer)

When the family walked into church, Father Michael welcomed them along with all the other families. Marcos said to his grandfather, "Abuelo, this is our pastor, Father Michael. He's going to celebrate the sacrament with us."

Then Luz pointed out the banner near the altar. She said, "Abuelo, Marcos and I helped make the banner."

Then their grandfather told the twins, "That is a very special banner. Now let's sit down and pray until the celebration begins."

I am preparing to celebrate the Sacrament of Penance for the first time. The people who will celebrate with me are ...

📖 Luke 7:36–50

Reader 1: In Jesus' time when people had guests come to their homes, they would ask the servants to wash their guests' feet.

Reader 2: One day a man named Simon invited Jesus to dinner. But when Jesus entered the house, no one offered to wash his feet.

Reader 3: During dinner a woman from the town came in and knelt by Jesus at the table. The woman cried so hard that her tears washed the dirt from Jesus' feet. Simon thought she was a sinner. He asked Jesus why he had let a sinner wash his feet.

Reader 4: Jesus answered, "When I entered your house, you did not give me water for my feet, but she has bathed them with her tears. So I tell you, her many sins have been forgiven." (Luke 7:44, 47)

Reader 5: Then Jesus said to the woman, "Your sins are forgiven. Your faith has saved you; go in peace." (Luke 7:48, 50)

59

We Believe and Celebrate

We all need God's forgiveness and love. So our parish community often gathers to celebrate the Sacrament of Penance together. This is what we do.

✦ We sing a song together. Then we are welcomed by the priest.

✦ We listen to readings from the Bible. These readings are about God's love and forgiveness.

✦ The priest talks to us about the readings.

✦ We listen to questions that are part of an examination of conscience. We think about the choices we have made.

✦ We say an act of contrition together. We tell God we are sorry for our sins and that we will try not to sin again. Then together we pray the Our Father.

When We Celebrate

Through the Sacrament of Holy Orders, a man becomes a priest. Many priests serve in local parishes. They spend their lives sharing God's love with people. They act in the Person of Christ in celebrating Mass and other sacraments.

During the Sacrament of Penance, we will see the priest wearing a purple stole. Since purple is a sign of penance, it helps us to remember to show our sorrow for sin by doing the penance the priest gives us.

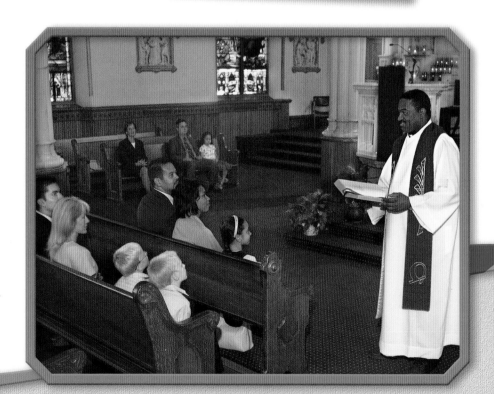

- Each person goes alone to tell his or her sins to the priest.

- The priest gives a penance to each person.

- Each person receives absolution. The priest stretches his right hand over each person's head and says the words of absolution. In God's name each person's sins are forgiven by the priest.

- Together we all praise and thank God for his mercy.

- The priest blesses the parish community. He tells all of us to "Go in peace."

Go in Peace

Sometimes you will celebrate the Sacrament of Penance individually with the priest.

Here is what happens when you celebrate the sacrament this way.

- ✦ The priest welcomes you, and you both make the sign of the cross.

- ✦ You listen as the priest shares a Bible story about God's forgiveness.

- ✦ You confess your sins to the priest.

- ✦ You and the priest talk about making right choices.

- ✦ The priest gives a penance to you. You will do your penance after the celebration of the sacrament.

- You pray an act of contrition. You tell God you are sorry for your sins and that you will try not to sin again.

- You receive absolution. The priest stretches his right hand over your head and says the words of absolution. In God's name your sins are forgiven by the priest.

- You and the priest praise and thank God for his love and forgiveness.

- The priest tells you, "Go in peace."

We Respond

I will thank the people who helped me prepare for First Penance by ...

I will celebrate First Penance on

_____.

Thank You

Here is my family's banner design for First Penance …

We Respond in Prayer

✝ **Leader:** Let us pray and sing together.

All: Hear us, Lord,
for you are merciful and kind.
In your great compassion,
look on us with love.
Amen.

🎵 We Come to Ask Forgiveness

Chorus
We come to ask your forgiveness, O Lord,
and we seek forgiveness from each other.
Sometimes we build up walls instead of
   bridges to peace,
and we ask your forgiveness, O Lord.

Sometimes we hurt
   by what we do to others.
Sometimes we hurt
   with words that are untrue.
Sometimes we cause others pain
   by what we fail to do,
and we ask your forgiveness, O Lord. (Chorus)

For the times when we've been
   rude and selfish,
for the times when we have been unkind;
and for the times we refused
   to help our friends in need,
we ask your forgiveness,
   O Lord. (Chorus)

We Are Peacemakers

"Make us living signs of your love."

Rite of Penance

We Gather

Justin and Alex were on the same soccer team. Last month after a game, Justin yelled at Alex and made fun of him for missing a goal. Alex was very upset. He walked away and went home.

Justin and Alex did not make up with each other. Each boy seemed to want his teammates to side with him. And some of the teammates did choose sides.

Then one day before practice, Mrs. Diaz, the coach, said, "Boys and girls, next week is the championship game. You have not been playing together as a team. What seems to be the problem?"

Someone explained what had happened.

Mrs. Diaz said, "Justin and Alex, it's time you two made up with each other. Your problem has hurt all of us. Everyone on the team needs to work together. Then we will have a chance at winning the championship game."

Justin and Alex thought about what their coach had said. They decided

_____

_____.
(fill in your answer)

This is how I work together with others...

📖 Matthew 5:1–2, 9

Reader 1: One day a very large crowd of people gathered to see Jesus. Jesus went up to the top of a mountain to teach. He knew that doing this would help everyone in the crowd to see and hear him.

Reader 2: Jesus said that day,

"Blessed are the peacemakers,
   for they will be called children of God."
(Matthew 5:9)

Jesus told us that he wants us to be peacemakers, too. We are peacemakers when we ask others to forgive us. We are also peacemakers when we forgive others.

71

We Believe and Celebrate

At the end of the celebration of the Sacrament of Penance, the priest tells us, "Go in peace." We go in peace because we have been forgiven. Then as soon as we can, we do the penance the priest has given us. The penance may be to say a prayer or prayers. The penance may also be to do a kind act. When we do a penance, we show that we are sorry for our sins.

Through the Sacrament of Penance:

◆ we are filled with God's grace

◆ we are joined to God and the Church

◆ God takes away punishment for our sins

◆ we receive peace and comfort

◆ we are strengthened to love God.

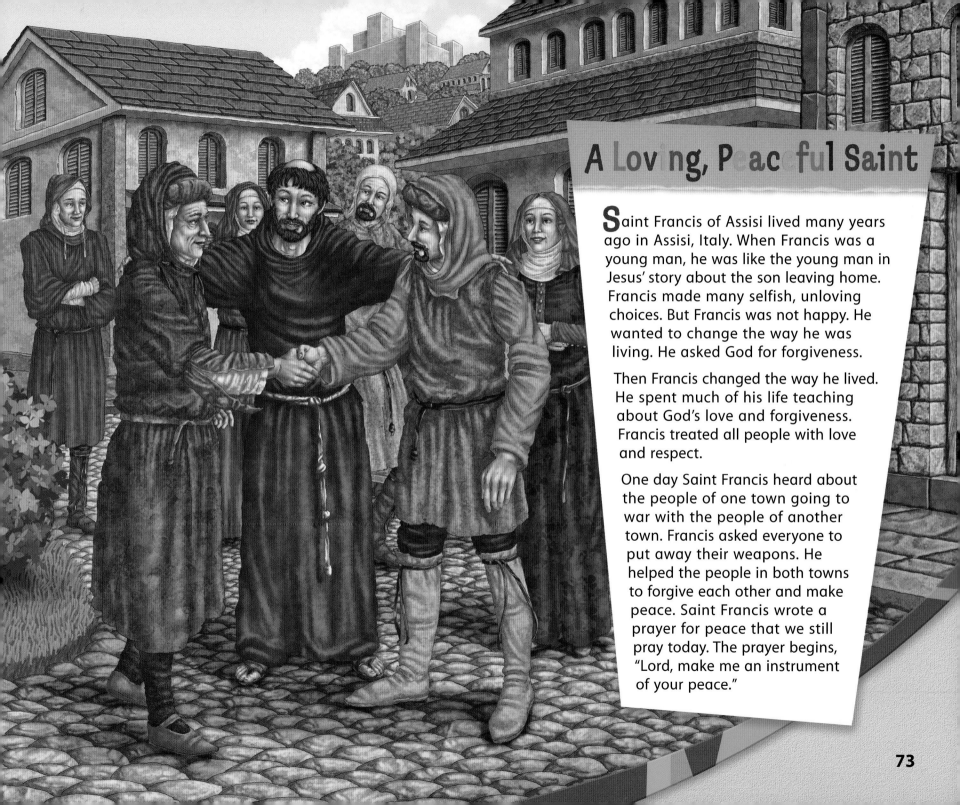

A Loving, Peaceful Saint

Saint Francis of Assisi lived many years ago in Assisi, Italy. When Francis was a young man, he was like the young man in Jesus' story about the son leaving home. Francis made many selfish, unloving choices. But Francis was not happy. He wanted to change the way he was living. He asked God for forgiveness.

Then Francis changed the way he lived. He spent much of his life teaching about God's love and forgiveness. Francis treated all people with love and respect.

One day Saint Francis heard about the people of one town going to war with the people of another town. Francis asked everyone to put away their weapons. He helped the people in both towns to forgive each other and make peace. Saint Francis wrote a prayer for peace that we still pray today. The prayer begins, "Lord, make me an instrument of your peace."

We Believe and Celebrate

On the night before he died, Jesus said, "Peace I leave with you; my peace I give to you." (John 14:27)

On that same night, Jesus also promised his disciples that the Holy Spirit would come to be our Helper. The Holy Spirit came to the Church on Pentecost. God the Holy Spirit is with the Church to guide us.

The Holy Spirit helps people of all ages to make loving, peaceful choices. Read about some of the peaceful choices made by children who are your age.

✦ At lunchtime Caroline asked a new student to sit with her and her friends. They helped the new student feel welcome in their group.

✦ Alberto's younger brother and sister were fighting with each other. Alberto helped them to make up with each other.

Place your picture here.

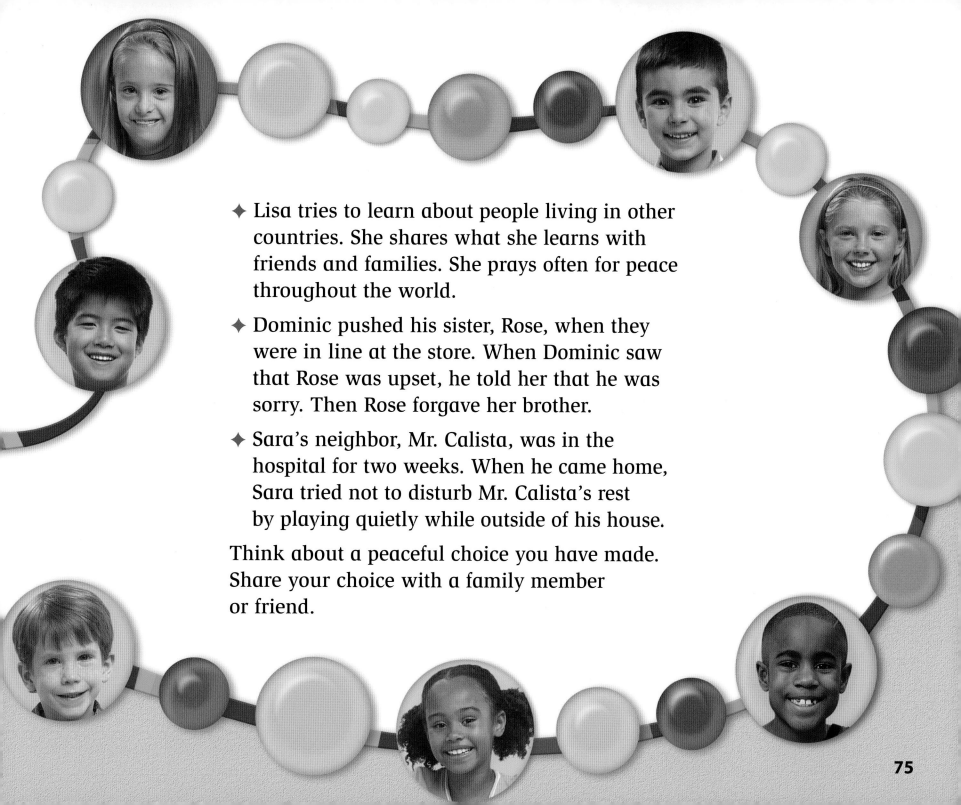

✦ Lisa tries to learn about people living in other countries. She shares what she learns with friends and families. She prays often for peace throughout the world.

✦ Dominic pushed his sister, Rose, when they were in line at the store. When Dominic saw that Rose was upset, he told her that he was sorry. Then Rose forgave her brother.

✦ Sara's neighbor, Mr. Calista, was in the hospital for two weeks. When he came home, Sara tried not to disturb Mr. Calista's rest by playing quietly while outside of his house.

Think about a peaceful choice you have made. Share your choice with a family member or friend.

Here are people who are peacemakers …

They share God's gift of peace by …

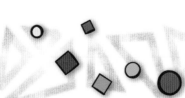

Here are some ways my family can share God's gift of peace ...

We Respond in Prayer

♫ **God Has Made Us a Family**

God has made us a family,
and together we will grow in love.
God has made us a family,
and together we will grow in love.

Oh yes! We need one another,
as together we grow in love;
and we will forgive one another,
as together we grow in love.

Place Your Family
Photo Here

✝ **Leader:** Let us listen to what Jesus taught us about God's gifts of forgiveness and peace.

Reader: "Blessed are the peacemakers, for they will be called children of God." (Matthew 5:9)

All: Holy Spirit, help us do what Jesus asked us to do. Help us to forgive others. Help us to share God's peace in our home, our parish, and our neighborhood.

Leader: Holy Spirit, we pray for peace throughout the world. Let us share a sign of peace with one another.

All: Lord, make us instruments of your peace.

The Ten Commandments

	Ways to Follow the Commandments
1. I am the LORD your God: you shall not have strange gods before me.	We believe that there is only one God.
2. You shall not take the name of the LORD your God in vain.	We speak God's name only with love and respect.
3. Remember to keep holy the LORD's Day.	We join our parish each week for Mass on Sunday or Saturday evening and holy days of obligation.
4. Honor your father and your mother.	We obey our parents and all who care for us.
5. You shall not kill.	We respect all human life.
6. You shall not commit adultery.	We respect our bodies and the bodies of others.
7. You shall not steal.	We take care of what we own and share with those in need.
8. You shall not bear false witness against your neighbor.	We tell the truth.
9. You shall not covet your neighbor's wife.	We show that we are happy and thankful for our family and friends.
10. You shall not covet your neighbor's goods.	We show that we are happy and thankful for what we own.

Celebrating Penance Individually

First I examine my conscience.
The priest greets me.
We both make the sign of the cross.

The priest asks me to trust in God's mercy.
The priest or I may read from the Bible.

I talk with the priest and I confess my sins.
The priest talks to me about loving God and others.
He gives me a penance.
I pray an act of contrition.

In the name of God and the Church, the priest gives me absolution:
The priest extends his hand over my head.
Through the words and actions of the priest, I receive God's forgiveness of my sins.

Together the priest and I give thanks for God's forgiveness.
I am sent to go in peace and to do the penance the priest gave me.

Celebrating Penance with the Community

We sing an opening hymn.
The priest greets us.
The priest prays an opening prayer.
We listen to a reading from the Bible and a homily.

We listen to questions that help us to examine our conscience.
Together we pray an act of contrition.
We may say a prayer or sing a song.
Then we pray the Our Father.

I meet individually with a priest to confess my sins.
The priest gives me a penance.
The priest gives me absolution.

After everyone has met individually with a priest, we thank God together for loving and forgiving us.
The priest says a concluding prayer to thank God.
The priest blesses us.
We are sent to go in peace and do the penance the priest gave to each of us.

"You shall love the Lord, your God, with all your heart."

(Matthew 22:37)

Talk about what Jesus told us to do when he gave us the Great Commandment.

① Sharing What I Learned

Look at the pictures and statements below. Match them. Use each match to tell your family what you learned in this chapter.

Our conscience is a gift from God to help us make the right choices

We can show our love for God by joining our parish each week at Mass.

When we follow the Great Commandment, we live as God's children.

Write the missing words in the puzzle.

Across

1. _____ gave special laws to his people because he loved them.

3. Jesus gave us the Great Commandment to teach us to _____ God, ourselves and others.

Down

2. Jesus said to love _____ as yourself.

1. G	**2.** O	D	
	t		
	h		
3. l	o	v	e
	r		
	s		

"Rejoice with me because I have found my lost sheep."

(Luke 15:6)

Talk about what the shepherd did after he found the lost sheep.

② Sharing What I Learned

Look at the pictures and statements below. Match them. Use each match to tell your family what you learned in this chapter.

Jesus our Good Shepherd leads us to reconciliation with God and others.

In Baptism, original sin and all other sins are taken away.

In the Sacrament of Penance we ask for and receive God's forgiveness of our sins.

Complete the sentences. Find the words in the letter box.

reconciliation is a word that means "coming back together again."

sin is any thought, word or act that we freely choose to commit even though it is wrong.

grace is God's life in us

Original sin is taken away in

Baptism.

C	X	O	C	R	J	L
P	T	O	R	E	U	H
M	G	R	A	C	E	Q
M	E	M	S	O	A	I
S	B	C	D	N	E	N
B	B	E	S	C	L	S
B	A	P	T	I	S	M
P	B	Q	D	L	I	O
I	E	Z	U	I	N	Y
R	A	Y	W	A	O	S
A	E	R	T	T	W	N
Y	A	C	N	I	K	J
D	S	X	O	O	C	L
P	T	O	R	N	U	H

"Father, I have sinned."

(Luke 15:21)

Talk about what the father did when he saw his younger son returning home.

3 Sharing What I Learned

Look at the pictures and statements below. Match them. Use each match to tell your family what you learned in this chapter.

As we prepare to celebrate the Sacrament of Penance, we make an examination of conscience.

God wants us to show respect for him, ourselves and others.

An act of contrition is a special prayer to tell God we are sorry for the wrong choices we have made.

Find the word missing for the sentence. Color the "X" spaces to find the clue.

I am _____ for my sins with all my heart.

4

"Zaccheus, come down quickly, for today I must stay at your house."

(Luke 19:5)

Talk about what Zacchaeus said he would do to show Jesus he was sorry.

87

Look at the pictures and statements below. Match them. Use each match to tell your family what you learned in this chapter.

In the Sacrament of Penance, the priest may read a story from the Bible. He talks to us about what we can do to make right choices.

In the Sacrament of Penance we confess our sins to the priest.

God forgives our sins through the words and actions of the priest. This is called absolution.

Use the code. Find the words to complete the sentence.

①	②	③	④	⑤	⑥	⑦
E	J	N	R	S	U	V

In the Sacrament of Penance, the priest is acting in

J E S U S
—— —— —— —— ——' name.
2 1 5 6 5

The priest will N E V E R
——————— —— —— —— —— ——
3 1 7 1 4

tell anyone the sins we confess.

88

"Your sins are forgiven. Your faith has saved you; go in peace."

(Luke 7:48, 50)

Talk about what Jesus said to:
• Simon
• the woman.

5 Sharing What I Learned

Look at the pictures and statements below. Match them. Use each match to tell your family what you learned in this chapter.

A parish community can gather together to celebrate the Sacrament of Penance.

The priest stretches his right hand over each person's head and says the words of absolution.

At the end of the celebration, the priest tells you to "go in peace."

During the Sacrament of Penance, the priest wears a purple stole. Color and decorate the priest's stole to help you remember that purple is a sign of penance.

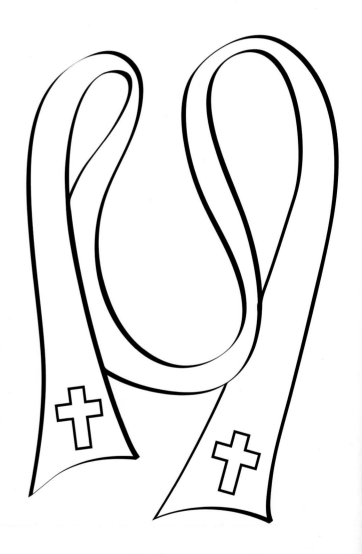

"Blessed are the peacemakers
for they will be called
children of God."

(Matthew 5:9)

Talk about what Jesus wants us
to do as peacemakers.

Sharing What I Learned

Look at the pictures and statements below. Match them. Use each match to tell your family what you learned in this chapter.

After celebrating the sacrament we do the penance the priest gave us.

The Holy Spirit helps people to make loving, peaceful choices.

Saint Francis helped people to forgive each other and make peace.

Make a storyboard about a peaceful choice you can make.

92

Sign of the Cross

In the name of the Father,
and of the Son,
and of the Holy Spirit. Amen.

Our Father

Our Father, who art in heaven,
hallowed be thy name;
thy kingdom come;
thy will be done on earth
  as it is in heaven.
Give us this day our daily bread;
and forgive us our trespasses
as we forgive those
  who trespass against us;
and lead us not into temptation,
but deliver us from evil.
Amen.

Glory to the Father

Glory to the Father, and to the Son,
    and to the Holy Spirit:
As it was in the beginning,
    is now, and will be for ever. Amen.

Hail Mary

Hail Mary, full of grace,
the Lord is with you!
Blessed are you among women,
and blessed is the fruit
    of your womb, Jesus.
Holy Mary, Mother of God,
pray for us sinners,
now and at the hour of our death.
Amen.

Act of Contrition

My God,
I am sorry for my sins with all my heart.
In choosing to do wrong
and failing to do good,
I have sinned against you
whom I should love above all things.
I firmly intend, with your help,
to do penance,
to sin no more,
and to avoid whatever leads me to sin.
Our Savior Jesus Christ
suffered and died for us.
In his name, my God, have mercy.

Morning Prayer

My God, I offer you today
All that I think and do and say,
Uniting it with what was done,
On earth, by Jesus Christ, your Son.

Evening Prayer

Dear God, before I sleep
I want to thank you for this day,
so full of your kindness and your joy.
I close my eyes to rest,
safe in your loving care.

Prayer for Peace

Lord, make me an instrument of your peace:
where there is hatred, let me sow love;
where there is injury, pardon;
where there is doubt, faith;
where there is despair, hope;
where there is darkness, light;
where there is sadness, joy.

O divine Master, grant that I may not so much seek
to be consoled as to console,
to be understood as to understand,
to be loved as to love.
For it is in giving that we receive,
it is in pardoning that we are pardoned,
it is in dying that we are born to eternal life.
Amen.

Saint Francis of Assisi